The Brief History of World War 2

The Rise of Adolf Hitler, Nazi Germany and the
Third Reich, Allied Forces, and the Battles from
Blitzkriegs to Atom Bombs

(1939-1945)

Disclaimer

Introduction

World **War II** was the escalation of the Second Sino-Japanese War that began in 1937 and a European war begun in 1939 into a military conflict fought from 1941 to 1945 on a global scale between two alliances: the Axis powers and the Allies. In the West, the years 1939 and 1945 are usually kept as the beginning and end of the war.

The First World War ended in 1918 with a victory for the three great western democracies: the United Kingdom, the Third French Republic and the United States. However, they did not form a formal military alliance thereafter. The UK and US disbanded most of their armed forces. This allowed the rise of aggressive authoritarian regimes: the communist Soviet Union in 1918, fascist Italy in 1922, a Japanese military dictatorship after 1926 and Nazi Germany in 1933. Eventually all countries became involved in an arms race accompanied by rising international tensions.

On 7 July 1937, Japan invaded China. After conquering the northeast of that country, a protracted war followed that claimed millions of victims. In the summer of 1939 the

Soviet Union defeated Japan when it tried to conquer Mongolia. Japan then decided to focus on the conquest of Southeast Asia. The National Socialist dictator of Germany, Adolf Hitler, had the demilitarized Rhineland occupied in 1936. In 1938, Germany annexed Austria in the *Anschluss*. In the Munich Treaty, Czechoslovakia had to cede the German-speaking Sudetenland. When Czechoslovakia was completely subjugated in March 1939, the UK and France promised to assist Poland in the event of a German attack. They hoped that Hitler would now refrain from an invasion because the German army was far from completing its build-up. On August 23, however, he concluded the Molotov-Ribbentrop Pact with the Soviet Union, which made him believe that an international intervention would not occur this time either.

The German Wehrmacht and the SS invaded Poland on September 1, 1939. The United Kingdom and France declared war to Germany on September 3, 1939. Poland was conquered after a month. The Soviet Union occupied the east of the country. British and French began to gather a surplus of men and equipment to defeat Germany in 1941. In April 1940, however, the Germans captured Denmark and Norway. In May 1940, the Low Countries

3

and France were defeated by a surprise advance of tank units through the Ardennes to the English Channel. The British repelled an invasion in the Battle of Britain. The US then offered material support to the UK, including the Loan and Lease Act. Germany tried to starve the UK by a submarine war and was itself bombed more and more intensively, all without decisive results. June 1940 Italy joined the war. Failed Italian attacks on Egypt and Greece forced Germany to engage in a subjugation of the entire Balkans and a protracted North African Campaign.

Hitler believed in 1941 that an "invincible" Wehrmacht could achieve the ideals of Nazi ideology: the extermination of the Jews and the subjugation of the Slavic *Untermenschen* to an upper layer of Germanic colonizers On June 22, 1941, Germany invaded the Soviet Union. After gaining great ground, this offensive ran aground in the autumn. On December 7, 1941, flying camp ships of the Japanese Empire carried out a surprise attack on the United States Pacific Fleet at Pearl Harbor. Four days later Hitler declared war on the US, the largest economy in the world. Thus the Axis powers became involved in a global conflict against a coalition whose military production already exceeded theirs many times over in 1942, so that their defeat was only a matter of time. That year they had further successes that ended in painful setbacks. Japan conquered large parts of Asia but suffered a decisive defeat at the Battle of Midway. German armies advanced into Egypt and into the oil fields of the Caucasus but were destroyed in the Second Battle of El Alamein and the Battle of Stalingrad. July 1943 a last major German offensive on the Eastern Front failed in the Battle of Kursk. That same month the British and Americans landed in Italy. The Italian dictator Benito Mussolini was overthrown. The Germans occupied northern Italy. Until May 1944 the Red Army could recapture the Ukraine because Hitler ordered a major part of his armoured reserves to be deployed in France. Nevertheless, the Western Allies managed to land in Normandy on D-Day, June 6, 1944, to finally break out and destroy a large part of the German army. They liberated France and Belgium. At the same time, the Red Army destroyed the German Army Group Middle in Operation Bagration. Finland, Romania and Bulgaria went over to the Allied side. The Wehrmacht was unable to recover from the losses suffered. The Allied advance was slowed by supply problems, the failure of Operation Market Garden and the German Ardennes Offensive. January 1945, the Weichsel-Oder Offensive crushed the German troops in Poland. The Allies moved west across the Rhine to make contact at the Elbe in May with the Red Army that had captured Berlin. Hitler had committed suicide. Germany capitulated on 8/9 May 1945.

A cooperation developed between the Soviet Union on the one hand and the British and Americans on the other hand, which was characterized by a lot of mutual unfamiliarity and mistrust, to which the Germans responded. This cooperation would soon turn into a new period of conflict after the end of World War II, known as the Cold War. Important, partly experiential, developments after the war were the establishment of the United Nations - which replaced the League of Nations that had proved powerless - and the drafting of the Universal Declaration of Human Rights.

Title

Already in 1939, after the British-French declaration of war to Germany because of the invasion of Poland, the term *Second World War* was used by the British conservative politician Duff Cooper, who in 1940 would be appointed by the new Prime Minister Winston Churchill as Minister *of* Information.

Only after 1945 would this designation become common, as would the designation *World War I* for the events of 1914-1918, previously referred to as the *Great War*, although it had already been used in 1918 by Charles à Court Repington.

Belgium and The Netherlands

Belgium and the Netherlands were attacked by Germany on 10 May 1940. On May 14, the Dutch army surrendered. The capitulation agreement was signed on 15 May. The capitulation did not apply to the province of Zeeland, where fighting continued for several days. Belgium capitulated after eighteen days of resistance on 28 May. The subsequent occupation lasted until 17 September 1944 in Belgium and until 6 May 1945 in the Netherlands north of the major rivers. Japan invaded the Dutch East Indies on 10 January 1942 and capitulated on 15 August 1945. The Netherlands would never regain full control of the island kingdom, which became independent in 1949.

Table of contents

Causes of war in Europe

The struggle for European hegemony 1866 - 1918

Following the establishment of the German Empire in 1871, German military and economic power increased rapidly, supported by further population growth and industrial development.

The German Confederation and North German Confederation, under Prussian leadership, had already won the Second German-Danish War (1864) and the Austro-Prussian War (1866). The rapid defeat of France in the Franco-German War in 1870-71, after which Germany annexed most of Alsace and Lorraine, made it clear that the balance of power in Europe had changed radically since the Napoleonic Wars.

The annexation caused a continuing serious territorial dispute between Germany and France.

A clumsy foreign policy under Wilhelm II of Germany also created tensions between the German Empire and both the United Kingdom and the Russian Empire. A factor for the British was that Germany was increasingly developing into a maritime and industrial rival.

They feared above all the dumping of German goods on the British market. For the Russians the stumbling block was the German support for Austria-Hungary in the Balkans, where the Dual Monarchy also dominated Slavic peoples. British, French and Russians began to form an anti-German bloc, the Triple Entente. This reinforced the

feelings of backwardness in Germany where an increasingly virulent nationalism, militarism and expansionism claimed for the country a hegemony that matched its position as the strongest land power in the world.

When rising tensions in 1914 led to the First World War, German military superiority proved insufficient for a quick victory. A bloody stalemate developed on the Western Front.

An Allied blockade of Germany caused severe shortages of raw materials for industry and famine. Fighting a war on two fronts was too great a burden. However, the Germans were not willing to make peace without territorial gains. The German secret service sent Lenin to Russia.

His new Soviet regime concluded the Peace of Brest-Litovsk. With the Spring Offensive of 1918, the German general staff hoped to achieve victory in the West before the Americans, who had come to their aid, could build up a superpower in 1919. At the same time they occupied the Ukraine to improve food supplies. This extreme effort only led to a rapid total exhaustion of the German army, followed by the November Revolution.

On 11 November 1918 Germany was forced to conclude an armistice. At that moment the frontline still crossed Belgium and that would give fuel to the dagger attack legend, that the front troops were betrayed by defeatist politicians.

The Treaty of Versailles in 1919 did not create a stable situation. The German population felt unfairly treated because of enormous reparations and territorial losses. Partly German-speaking areas fell to France (Alsace and Lorraine) or Poland, which had been independent again since 1793.

East Prussia was isolated from the rest of Germany by the Danzig corridor. This led to revanchism and irredentism. The Allies were given no compelling guarantees to prevent a German resurrection. The German army was reduced in size and armament but not disbanded. Only the Rhineland was occupied and against the wishes of France not permanently but only for fifteen years. The French Marshal Ferdinand Foch therefore described the Treaty of

Versailles as "not a peace, but an armistice of twenty years".

German instability 1918 - 1929

After the armistice, politically unstable Germany fell prey to chaos and poverty. Left and right fought for power. This battle would eventually be settled in favour of totalitarian National Socialism. The essence of this fascist movement was that the stronger has the right to dominate the weaker. This explains both the radical nationalist, anti-Semitic, militaristic, anti-democratic and anti-communist character of this movement and the ideologically inspired war of annihilation that ensued. However, this process lasted fifteen years.

The social democratic, liberal and Christian democratic middle parties of the Weimar Republic attempted to establish a democratic constitutional state, but were immediately confronted with uprisings. The Russian Communist October Revolution of 1917 led to a wave of revolution throughout Europe. In Bavaria the communists proclaimed a council republic in early 1919 and in Berlin there was the Spartacus revolt. Prime Minister Friedrich

Ebert saw himself forced to put down the uprisings with radical right-wing militias of returned front soldiers, the Free Corps.

These nationalistic groups did not realize that Germany could be responsible for its own misery, although they did not fight hard enough.

Alleged "traitors" like Foreign Minister Walther Rathenau and ex-Vice Chancellor Matthias Erzberger were killed by right-wing terror. The old regime of nobility, bureaucracy and army had lost all authority, as evidenced by the Kapp-putsch, a revolt by Freikorps against the disbanding of their army units, which culminated in a failed coup attempt.

In the general election of June 1920, the far left (Unabhängige Sozialdemokratische Partei Deutschlands) and far right wing (German-nationals) won at the expense of the centre. Right-wing groups of conservatives and nationalists, however, did not want to assume governmental responsibility.

When in 1922 the situation in Germany started to stabilise a little, the country was imposed a huge reparation payment of 136 billion marks, which it had no chance to pay. France and Belgium, without the support of England and America, occupied the Ruhr area, where industrial production came to a standstill.

Combined with monetary financing, the printing of unbacked money, this led to hyperinflation that made the savings of the middle class worthless.

The new director of the Rijksbank, Hjalmar Schacht, ended inflation by equating twenty billion old marks to one new mark. The new currency gained value through huge loans provided by the United States and Dutch banks, which lent three billion marks.

This allowed the circulation of money to resume and made it possible for Germany to make reparations. With that, France and the United Kingdom repaid their debts to the United States.

Shortly afterwards, in 1923, a right-wing coup attempt in Bavaria, the Bierkellerputsch, failed. At the time it attracted little attention but one of the participants was Adolf Hitler of the National Socialist German Workers' Party.

Hitler was sentenced to five years in prison, a year of which he eventually had to serve. During this imprisonment he dictated *Mein Kampf*, which would later occupy a central place in Nazi propaganda.

In 1924, somewhat better times came for Germany. Gustav Stresemann, German Minister of Foreign Affairs during the presidency of Hindenburg (1925 - 1934), sought a rapprochement with the western countries. Charles Dawes as chairman of an international commission drew up the Dawes Plan, a payment scheme for German reparations. Prime Ministers Ramsay MacDonald and Édouard Herriot agreed to the Dawes Plan, and Germany also agreed. In 1925 Germany concluded the Treaty of Locarno with France, Britain and a number of other neighbouring countries. The Ruhr troops were withdrawn and the new western borders were mutually guaranteed. It also paved the way for a membership in the League of Nations, which would take place in 1926.

May 1928 the German people clearly opted for a peace policy by giving the Social Democrats an election victory while Hitler received only 2.5 percent of the votes. On August 27, 1928, Minister Stresemann signed the Briand-

Kellogg pact in Paris, together with other major powers. International disputes were not to be solved by war, but by peaceful means such as arbitration.

However, the Weimar Republic did not act in good faith in this matter. Germany was forbidden to possess tanks, but this was circumvented by secret weapon development in Sweden and the Soviet Union.

In the spring of 1929, American diplomat Owen D. Young came up with the Young plan. It eased payments to 114 billion to be met over 59 years, equal to about 3% of GNP. The Germans had expected a much larger reduction.

The German National People's Party presented it as an unbearable burden on the German people and grew in popularity. A referendum (*Volksentscheid*) rejected the plan by a large majority but was not binding.

The German government accepted the plan at the First Hague Restoration Conference and the Second Hague Restoration Conference of 1930, mainly because it now had the right to suspend reparations for two years. The prospect of this destabilized the entire international financial system as early as the summer of 1929.

18

Great Depression

The 1929 stock market crash caused the US economy to collapse. The American banks demanded their loans in Europe. Governments everywhere turned to protectionism, restricting imports, causing world trade to collapse. The Great Depression was a fact. Germany was hit hard. The cabinet of Heinrich Brüning, who took office in March 1930, reacted with severe budget cuts, combined with plans for rearmament by general Kurt von Schleicher.

In elections in September 1930, the NSDAP won 18.5% of the votes. In June 1931, Brüning suspended reparations, leading to an international bank run. Unemployment rose from two to six million between 1929 and 1933, 30% of the labor force.

In 1932, the Lausanne Conference exempted Germany from further reparations, but this had become an unimportant issue in light of the fundamental crisis it faced.

The communists advocated the introduction of a planned economy so that the state could put the idle factories back to work. The middle class, however, feared such a Bolshevik takeover of power.

19

An alternative was the NSDAP with its mixture of socialism and nationalism. The number of NSDAP voters grew to almost fourteen million, 39.9% of the vote, at the July 1932 elections. The *Sturmabteilung* intimidated opponents.

However, President Paul von Hindenburg refused to appoint Hitler as Reich Chancellor. In the November 1932 elections the Nazis lost support. Chancellor Franz von Papen began to lead a very authoritarian regime.

In January 1933, von Papen and Alfred Hugenberg, the leader of the DNVP, persuaded Hindenburg to appoint Hitler as Chancellor of the Reich in a cabinet in which they would also have a seat.

On 27 February 1933 the Reichstag fire took place, which the Nazis used as an opportunity to use an emergency ordinance (the Reichstag fire ordinance) to persecute members of the left-wing parties without trial and imprison them in concentration camps.

In the Reichstag election of March 5, 1933, Hitler's party received 44% of the votes and Hugenberg's party received 8%. So Hitler did not have an absolute majority, but through persecution of the leftist parties and intimidation of

20

the others he had the Enabling Act passed and was able to seize power. Hitler banned all parties except the NSDAP himself and did not allow free elections, effectively ruling the country as a dictator.

1933 - 1939

Hitler's regime was economically very successful. By 1939 unemployment had been virtually eliminated and GNP almost doubled. The infrastructure, such as the road network, was greatly improved. This aspect of his regime received widespread support from the German people. However, the success was due to a managed wage policy.

Wages had collapsed in 1932 and were not allowed to rise after that. Strikes were prohibited. Much of the economic growth was swallowed up by the arms industry.

The regime could not live up to the claim that wealth was redistributed and more expensive consumer goods became available to the mass of the population. Hitler believed that an increase in purchasing power and further growth would depend on access to strategic raw materials and petroleum of which Germany had a structural lack.

21

There was, partly due to mounting budget deficits, always a shortage of foreign currency to buy it on the world market. Since hyperinflation, it was taboo to devalue the mark to promote exports.

Hitler also no longer wanted to be part of the international financial and economic system controlled by the US and UK. The alternative was to secure access to resources through wars of conquest.

22

That option suited the Nazi ideology much better. War was not only a means but also an end in itself. In the eternal struggle between the races, it was the historical destiny of the superior Aryan German *Herrenvolk* to subjugate and dominate the Slavic *Untermenschen*.

Despite intensive militaristic and racist indoctrination, however, the German people were certainly not in a war mood. The security services reported that, with the horrors of the previous world war still fresh in the memory, the enthusiasm for a new slaughter was low.

The *Wehrmacht* itself did not consider itself ready for military conflict until 1943. Versailles had limited the size of the Reichswehr to one hundred thousand men. Tanks and an air force were prohibited; the navy was allowed only lighter ships. March 1935 began an open rearmament. Despite increasing military spending, rising to 18% of GNP in 1938, it was difficult to catch up. Most of the money was spent on barracks, training and bunkers.

Not enough could be spent on expensive and rapidly aging heavy weapons. In mid 1939, the Wehrmacht had 9000 guns, 2500 tanks, 2300 aircraft, 57 submarines and 45

23

surface ships. In all these types of weapons were behind potential enemies. The armament led to a shortage of money that only seemed to be solved by a war of aggression but was still not enough to guarantee victory purely on numerical superiority.

Shortly after the war the theory was popular that the Nazis found a way out of this problem in the innovative tactics of *blitzkrieg*. There was even said to have been a "blitzkrieg strategy": by investing in tanks and concentrating them in a small number of high-end armoured divisions, the Nazis could defeat the enemy in a rapid modern fashion and thus gain world domination in an ultimately inexpensive manner. Although such campaigns were indeed conducted in the early years of the war, historical research in the 1950s revealed that such a strategy never existed.

Hitler had no elaborate plan to conquer the world and was only vaguely aware of the importance of armored units.

Later it also became clear that there was not even a blitzkrieg doctrine. In the German army were quite traditional and solid thinking dominant. Hitler was primarily an opportunist.

By striving to bring German-speaking regions *Heim ins Reich*, he tried to enthuse the German people for at least a limited conflict. Such an appeal to the right of nations to self-determination could also force concessions from the British and the French. They were sensitive to this because they thought they were threatened by a much more dangerous opponent than Germany.

25

By 1928, Joseph Stalin had seized all power in the Soviet Union. The country began a transformation into a superpower. The Red Army grew into the largest fighting force in the world. The United Kingdom and France feared that Stalin intended to unleash a world revolution.

They reinforced the *cordon sanitaire*, a chain of anti-communist states. As early as the early 1930s, they began to develop modern weapons more intensively. But in response to the Great Depression they were cutting back. They were unwilling to increase their defense budgets very rapidly. They hoped that a conservative and militarily strong German state could keep the Soviet Union in check.

Therefore they did not intervene when Germany announced a rearmament. January 1935 France ended its mandate over the Saarland. It did not intervene in March 1936 when the Rhineland, cleared by French troops in 1930 on condition of permanent demilitarization, was again occupied by German troops.

So the old Entente no longer maintained the international legal order. Also the US, with a minimal army and a population strongly in favour of isolationism, kept itself aloof. Aggressive countries now saw their chance. Germany left the League of Nations in 1933. In October 1935 Italy invaded Abyssinia.

July 1937 Japan invaded China. Germany allied itself with Japan in the Anti-Komintern Pact in 1936 and with Italy in the Rome-Berlin axis. These axis powers got an even closer bond in May 1939 in the Steel Pact. In March 1938, Germany forced Austria to annex in the *Anschluss*.

TERRITORIES OF POLAND ANNEXED
BY THE THIRD REICH AND THE SOVIET UNION
(Lines of partition from 10/21/1939 to 6/22/1941)

The increasingly powerful and radical Germany now began to inspire more fear in the UK and France than the Soviet Union despite its *proxy war* with the Axis in the Spanish Civil War. Stalin focused on his internal problems and fearing his own armed forces he largely exterminated its

28

officer corps. The British and French armed themselves vigorously.

Since they already had a large military infrastructure, much still usable artillery from the previous war, and the modern fortress belt of the Maginot Line, they knew they could take on Germany in short order.

When Hitler claimed the German-speaking Sudetenland from Czechoslovakia in the autumn of 1938, they considered going into battle.

Czechoslovakia was well armed and had a strong fortress belt; France could invade the Rhineland while the *Westwall* was still unfinished. British Prime Minister Neville Chamberlain, however, wanted to give *peace* another chance *in our time* and allowed the Munich Treaty to annex the Sudetenland to Germany.

This appeasement policy would fail. It only taught Hitler that he would be rewarded if he broke his promises. In March 1939, Hitler forced the rump state of Czechoslovakia to divide into the German Protectorate of Bohemia and Moravia and the First Slovak Republic, a vassal state.

29

The extensive Czech equipment and arms industry fell into his hands. The UK and France had had enough and gave military guarantees to Poland. The Poles rejected Hitler's demand to give up their German-speaking territories and become a vassal state. The German military leadership and many Nazi leaders feared a war because Germany was not ready for it. On 24 August, however, Hitler scored an enormous diplomatic victory.

The Entente had assumed that the Soviet Union would turn against its ideological enemy Nazi Germany anyway. Hitler, however, offered Stalin to divide Eastern Europe among himself in exchange for neutrality and supply of raw materials. They concluded the Molotov-Ribbentrop Pact. Hitler now assumed that the British and French would again refrain from a military reaction. On September 1 at 05:00 hours Germany invaded Poland. The UK and France announced that they would honor their treaty obligations to Poland.

On 2 September Italian Foreign Minister Galeazzo Ciano proposed a five-state conference at San Remo, following an armistice. The UK made it a condition that Germany would first withdraw its troops from Poland; when this was not forthcoming, the UK in the evening of 3 September and France in the night of 3 September addressed a formal declaration of war to Germany, making World War II an irrevocable fact.

The war in Europe

The invasion of Poland

Following the plan Fall Weiss, Germany invaded Poland on September 1, 1939. This invasion was a war of aggression in violation of the 1928 Briand-Kellogg pact, also signed by Germany. The apparent justification was the Gleiwitz-incident. The French had promised Poland to open a western front in Germany with sixty divisions, but in fact limited themselves to the weak Saar offensive with nine divisions. This allowed the Germans to launch a strong main attack from Silesia towards Warsaw. The Poles were weakened there because they had not yet fully mobilized their army not to provoke Hitler and had concentrated important forces around Poznań for a surprise attack towards Berlin. After several days of heavy fighting, the Polish front towards Silesia broke. However, the advancing German main force was then ambushed on the left flank by the Polish army in Posen. They managed to shake it off and destroy it, after which they laid siege to Warsaw. Meanwhile, German armoured forces had cut through the Danzig corridor to attack Warsaw from the east via East Prussia. Attempts to take the city by storm failed but after a

bombardment the capital capitulated on 28 September.
The Germans immediately began systematically murdering
all Polish intellectuals.

The Soviet Union invaded eastern Poland on 17
September 1939 under the pretext of protecting Belarusian
and Ukrainian minorities. Officially, the country remained
neutral. The fighting in Poland ended on October 6, 1939,
but the Polish Carpathian Army and the government fled
via Romania to France, where they set up fighting units
which had to flee again to England in 1940.

Twilight War

After October the French ended their offensive. After that there were hardly any combat contacts on the French-German border. Both sides refrained from strategic bombing. This twilight war, which would last until April 1940, was called in English the *phoney war* and in French the *drôle de guerre*; in German the *Sitzkrieg*.

However, the calm on the fronts masked feverish activity in preparing future campaigns. Germany offered peace but the Allies refused to accept the occupation of Poland. They hoped to exhaust their enemy by an economic blockade, as in World War I. However, Soviet supplies would make that difficult. Therefore, they turned to a real war economy to build up an excess of men and materiel to defeat Germany. In the UK, conscription had already been introduced in April 1939, and France, which had few recruits due to low birth rates, imported them *en masse* from North Africa. For the tens of thousands of tanks and planes they needed, they wanted to call on the largest industrial country in the world, the United States of America. American neutrality laws prohibited the supply of war materiel to a warring party, but on 5 November 1939,

President Franklin Delano Roosevelt introduced the system of *cash and carry*: those waging war were allowed to purchase weapons if they could pay for them immediately and transport them themselves. This greatly favoured the Entente because Germany could do neither. However, there was no hurry. They expected to be ready for an attack on Germany in the summer of 1941 at the earliest, and probably not until 1942, when the UK hoped to field fifty-five divisions, all motorized, the most modern fighting force in the world.

For the German military top it was a gloomy prospect. They foresaw that Germany would not be able to keep up with the pace of armament. There would be an acute shortage of money and strategic raw materials. In March 1940, German imports had shrunk by 80%. The best one could hope for was another stalemate, but such a protracted war would exhaust the country even more. Therefore, when Hitler ordered an attack on the West even before October, it was pointed out to him that ammunition had run out for the time being. Still, in the short term, the balance of power would shift slightly in Germany's favor. The attack on Poland had been made possible by some thirty highly professional divisions of the standing army, some six hundred thousand men. In haste, they had then begun training 1.1 million recruits and 1.7 million World War I veterans. When that was completed in the spring of 1940, Germany had acquired a large fighting force with which, by maneuvering, it might improve its position before the Allied buildup would have made their front unassailable. Germany's best tactician, Heinz Guderian, and strategist, Erich von Manstein, came up with a daring plan in the autumn of 1939. The army was to advance right through the Ardennes, cross the Meuse, and then make a deep strategic penetration with tanks into the English Channel. This type of attack, which would later come to be known as *Blitzkrieg*, had been much discussed in books before the war but was not accepted as a method by any army in 1939. The plan was brought to Hitler's attention and this forced Chief of Staff Franz Halder to at least adopt the Ardennes element, although the poor road network would make such an advance very risky. There was no alternative, however, according to him: without such a gamble one would lose anyway.

The Soviet expansion

By 1939, the Soviet Union had replaced Maksim Litvinov as Minister of Foreign Affairs with Vyacheslav Molotov, after which the country seemed to embark on an anti-Western course. The Soviet Union forced Estonia, Latvia and Lithuania to accept garrisons from the Red Army in 1939.

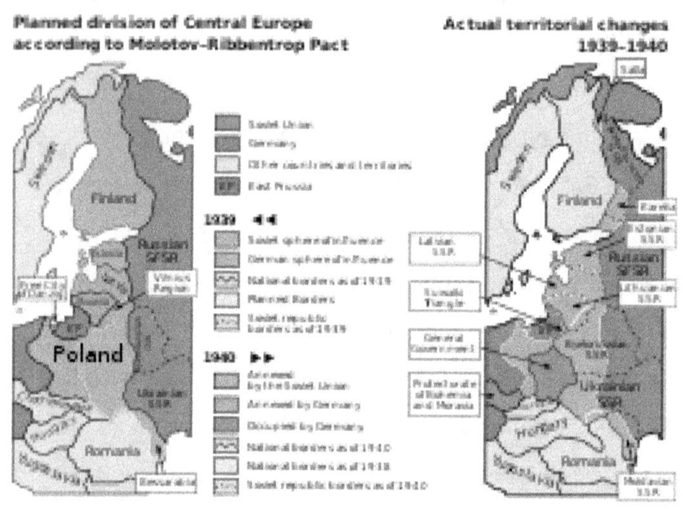

Actually in August 1939 it was agreed that Lithuania would fall within the German sphere of influence - March 1939 they already had to give up Memelland - but the country was exchanged for a strip of Polish territory which was added to the General Government, the Polish heartland which was not annexed by Great-Germany. Lithuania also received a strip of Polish territory, with the city of Vilnius.

Stalin wanted Finland to annex the Karelian isthmus, near Leningrad, the second city of the USSR, in exchange for a strip of Finnish territory in Eastern Karelia. The Finnish government refused because on the isthmus was the Mannerheim Line, which was essential for the Finnish defence.

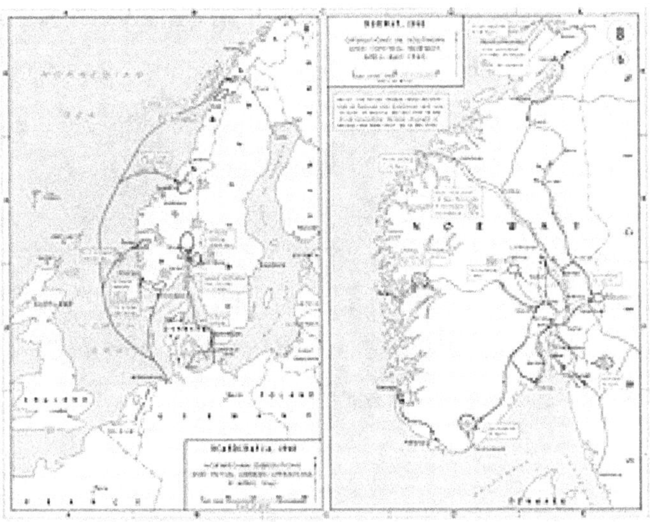

On 30 November 1939 the Red Army began an offensive to conquer Finland. In this Winter War they got stuck on
38

the Mannerheim Line while north of it on icy forest tracks armoured divisions were crushed by the Finns.

They lost two thousand tanks and two hundred thousand men against the Finns twenty-five thousand. The French cabinet now also considered declaring war on the Soviet Union and coming to the aid of the brave little country. At the same time old pro-Finnish sentiments revived in Germany.

Stalin then forced the Mannerheim Line with a large force and at the armistice of March 13, 1940 he settled for the isthmus and Eastern Karelia. The event seriously damaged the prestige of the Red Army and contributed greatly to the German underestimation of its military strength.

In 1940, after the fall of France, the Soviet Union annexed the Baltic States and Romania Bessarabia and Northern Bukovina. Hundreds of thousands of inhabitants of these areas were deported to the east.

Denmark and Norway

Norway was important to the German war effort as a supply route for Swedish iron ore, accounting for half of Germany's steel production, and a potential fleet base for the *Kriegsmarine*. The Germans therefore made plans for an invasion from the end of 1939, but so did the British, partly in connection with possible aid to Finland.

On Hitler's initiative Operation Weserübung was prepared, the occupation of Norway. At the end of February an invasion of Denmark was added. On 3 April 1940, the first supply ships left and on 6 April the German war fleet sailed to Norway. At the same time as the German invasion, the Allies planned an operation to lay mines in Norwegian waters to block the German supply route of iron ore. On 8 April, the British laid naval mines in the Vestfjord off Narvik. The Allies also planned limited landings in Norway to protect these minefields. However, the German invasion thwarted those plans.

The Germans landed on 9 April in Oslo, Bergen, Trondheim, Kristiansand, Egersund and Narvik. The landing in Oslo failed partially. Fort Oscarsborg first sank the heavy cruiser *Blücher* and then severely damaged the fortress battleship *Lützow*. The landing at Narvik was successful, but on 10 and 13 April ten German destroyers were sunk by counterattacks from the British fleet.On 15 April the British made landings in central Norway at Namsos and Åndalsnes. However, their expeditionary forces were defeated by the Germans. Counterattacks near Narvik, the main transit port for iron ore, were more successful. French and British troops recaptured the port. When France was threatened, the expeditionary force was evacuated. The airship *Glorious was sunk by the* battleships *Scharnhorst* and *Gneisenau*. The Norwegian army capitulated on June 9, 1940. King and government fled to England. The German surface fleet was seriously weakened by the losses.

On April 9, German troops crossed the Danish border and attacked Copenhagen. After two hours of battle, the Danish government surrendered before they had time to declare war on Germany. Officially Denmark remained an unoccupied neutral country with a small German garrison but also with its own king, cabinet, parliament and armed forces. On 12 April the British occupied the Faroe Islands and on 10 May Iceland, which was placed under American

41

administration in 1941. Later in 1941 Greenland also placed itself under American administration, even before the US became a war party. Denmark was placed under German military administration in August 1943. Iceland declared its independence in 1944.

The Western Campaign 1940

On 10 May 1940, the German Wehrmacht started to implement *Fall Gelb*, the plan to occupy the Netherlands, Belgium and Luxembourg in order to bomb England. They also blocked a possible advance route for the expected Entente offensives.

Because the Allies had a numerical superiority in men, tanks and artillery, they wanted a smart strategy to achieve victory. They hoped with a diversionary attack by Army Group B to lure the best British and French troops to the north to cut them off via the Ardennes.

The Dutch defences were caught off guard by extensive German airborne landings. An attack on The Hague failed but via the captured bridges at Moerdijk and Dordrecht, *9. Panzerdivision* entered the Fortress Holland. Heinkel He 111s carried out the bombardment of Rotterdam on 14 May and threatened to destroy Utrecht, whereupon Commander-in-Chief General Winkelman surrendered his troops in the Netherlands in the late afternoon, with the exception of Zeeland. On Wednesday morning, May 15, 1940, the military surrender agreement was signed. The government, Queen Wilhelmina and the navy fled to England.

The British Expeditionary Force and the French 7th and 1st Army united with the Belgian Army in central Belgium. Meanwhile Army Group A moved through the Ardennes. On 13 May continuous and massive bombardments broke the French main front at Sedan and German motorized infantry crossed the Meuse.

Contrary to Halder's plan, the German armoured generals like Guderian and Erwin Rommel now left the bridgeheads without waiting for reinforcements and, in the style of a

Blitzkrieg, carried out a strategic penetration to the Channel which was reached on 20 May.

However, a "half order" from Hitler, overwhelmed by success, prevented the immediate capture of Dunkirk and by 2 June, 330,000 British and French troops in the evacuation of Dunkirk managed to escape the siege, leaving behind their heavy equipment. However, the Belgian army surrendered on 28 May, ending its 18-day campaign. Leopold III of Belgium remained in the country but the government left.

The German success had been greater than they had dared to hope and they decided to exploit this by immediately defeating France as a whole according to the
45

plan *Fall Rot*. On 5 June an attack on the Somme began, followed on 9 June by a main offensive that tore open the centre of the French front. The tactic of strategic penetration had now been embraced by the German High Command. On 14 June Paris was declared an open city and on 17 June German tanks reached the Swiss border, encircling the Maginot Line. Italy declared war on 10 June, limiting itself to weak border fighting.

Germany easily could have conquered the whole of France, but Hitler wanted to come to an agreement with a French government to prevent the war from continuing from the colonies and to lure the British to peace. On 22 June 1940 France signed an armistice in which it ceded Alsace-Lorraine and the country was divided into a northern occupation zone and a southeastern puppet state Vichy-France, with the conservative-nationalist Marshal Philippe Pétain as head of state. However, General Charles de Gaulle had already announced on 18 June that he would continue the struggle as leader of the Free French; they had only a minimal following for the time being. In Rome on 24 June France ceded an 800 km² zone to Italy. On 3 July the British sank part of the French fleet

in the Attack on Mers-el-Kébir, fearing it would fall into
German hands.

The Battle of Britain

After the French defeat, Hitler waited in vain for a British peace offer. The new Prime Minister Winston Churchill, who succeeded Neville Chamberlain on May 10, 1940, wanted to continue the war. Although the British land forces were weak for the time being, the superiority of the Royal Navy, the largest fleet in the world, made a German invasion practically impossible. Hitler and the German Navy recognized this as well. Hoping to intimidate the British, he nevertheless ordered on 16 July 1940 to prepare Operation Seelöwe, a landing. Planning and landing craft were initially lacking. To stand a chance, the Luftwaffe, the best-equipped German armed forces, attempted to gain air superiority for nearly two months by eliminating Royal Air Force airfields in southern England. Because of the rapidly increasing British aircraft production and a new network of radar installations, it was very difficult. Both sides became exhausted.

The accidental bombing of a residential area of London on August 24, 1940, led to a British retaliatory attack on Berlin. Hitler ordered a massive bombing of London. From 7 September 1940 an attempt was made to break the

British will to war by systematic terrorist bombing of the civilian population, but this proved to be a fatal mistake. The thousands of casualties and the damage done in London and other cities did not break morale. Germany had no strategic bomber force and was physically unable to destroy England. The RAF recovered its airfields and inflicted increasingly heavy losses on the Germans. *Seelöwe* was delayed and eventually called off. The Luftwaffe had lost over 1500 aircraft, which would rise to 3132 by the end of March 1941.

For Churchill the success was a great boost. It proved that the Germans could be defeated and convinced the British population of the necessity and feasibility of a further battle. The heroic resistance got full sympathy from the American population and made it easier for Roosevelt to pursue a pro-British policy.

German and American strategy

The Fall of France came as a shock to the whole world. It represented a revolution in the geostrategic situation. France had had the reputation of being the strongest army in the world. That status now fell to Germany which was gaining hegemony on the European continent.

The Nazis saw it as the establishment of a New Order. The "decadent" liberal democracies were finished. The four great totalitarian dictatorships could divide the world, especially the British Empire, among themselves: Italy would have Africa, the Soviet Union would have India, and Japan would have Southeast Asia. However, no peaceful alliance would come about. The victory fed Hitler's delusions of grandeur.

He deluded himself that it was due to his genius as a field general. He started to believe in his own propaganda that the *Wehrmacht* was an "invincible war machine". Not wishing to remain dependent on supplies from Stalin, he ordered to prepare the subjugation of the Soviet Union already in June 1940. If the UK had made peace, he would have launched an attack in the east in September.

The German people were greatly relieved by the quick victory, with only a fraction of the number killed in the First World War. Hitler reached the height of his popularity.
51

People expected to reap the economic benefits in the sense of a higher standard of living. Luxury goods like coffee and cocoa, looted from France and the Low Countries, became available for a short time. However, further growth in prosperity was not to be expected. On the contrary, due to the transition to a war economy, the production of consumer goods decreased.

Food yields fell as fertilizer factories switched to the manufacture of explosives. Hitler tried to alleviate the pain by limiting military spending on the GNP to 38%, compared to the 60% that would be reached in 1943. This forced clear choices to be made in the use of limited production capacity. An expensive and uncertain plan to develop an atomic bomb was rejected at an early stage.

In a two-front war, Hitler wanted to simultaneously defeat the UK and the USSR. The former he hoped to do by building hundreds of submarines. In addition, the air force continued a 40% seizure of arms production.

Scarcity of iron ore and labour prevented the production of the tens of thousands of tanks that Guderian said would be needed for a possible long-term war in the east. It was therefore optimistically assumed that the new tactics of *Blitzkrieg* would guarantee a quick victory over the Red Army.

The Americans, too, were shocked. The population began to see Nazi Germany as a serious threat for the first time. Roosevelt came to believe that US participation in the war on the side of the UK was inevitable. However, he had to act cautiously because isolationism was still very strong. Early June 1940, by presidential order, he sent old stocks of guns and ammunition to the British. On 2 September he agreed with Churchill on the *Destroyers-for-bases deal*: in exchange for fifty old destroyers, very useful for convoy service, British bases in the western hemisphere were leased to the Americans. On September 16 the US introduced conscription. When Roosevelt was re-elected for the second time in November, he could act more openly in favor of the British. On December 29, in a radio talk show, he called the U.S. the "Arsenal of Democracy" and announced a massive weapons production program. Recommended as a means of getting the British to fight instead of Americans, it was in fact used primarily to turn the world's largest economy into a military superpower as well. On March 11, 1941, the Loan and Lease Act went into effect. This allowed the US government to lease fifty billion dollars worth of war materiel to other allies free of charge during the war. On 14 August 1941 the UK and the US concluded the Atlantic Charter in which they laid down their vision of the situation after the war. During the second half of 1941 American surface ships escorted convoys in the western Atlantic and attacked German submarines.

The Battle of the Atlantic

German submarines had already sunk the British airship *Courageous* and battleship *Royal Oak* in 1939. The UK's Achilles heel was the fact that 70% of its food had to be imported. An effective blockade could starve Britain. From 1940 the *Kriegsmarine*, using French ports and a growing number of submarines, tried to sink more British merchant ships than could be built.

Already in 1941 they were losing that race due to the effective system of sailing in escorted convoys. After the declaration of war on the US, the goal became completely impossible despite Operation Paukenschlag to hit American coastal shipping.

In May 1943, the number of German operational submarines reached a peak of 240. Allied losses were high but then declined rapidly with the introduction of sonar and radar systems to detect submarines, long-range air patrols, and the cracking of the Enigma codes to encrypt German military communications.

Although 3500 Allied merchant ships were eventually sunk in the Atlantic, the Germans lost 783 submarines. Their enormous investment in submarine weaponry had no noticeable positive impact on the course of the war.

Besides submarines, Germany could also use large surface ships, *raiders*, to hunt down Allied merchant shipping. But they did not have too many of those. After the battleship *Bismarck was lost* in May 1941, they did not venture west of the British Isles anymore. Until 1944 they did attack Allied convoys to Murmansk from the Norwegian fjords.

Air War

Unlike Germany, the United Kingdom mass-produced four-engine strategic bombers with a long flying range. From February 1941, it tried to hit German population centers and industries.

Well into 1944 this was the only possibility to attack Germany directly. The bombing had little effect at first, partly because of the need to operate only at night for safety's sake.

In 1942 the US joined the air war. The heavily armed B-17 Flying Fortress allowed the Americans to fly during the day. In 1943 the Allies were so strong that they could systematically destroy all German cities. This forced the

Germans to invest in a wide belt of radar installations, airfields and anti-aircraft guns, in France, the Low Countries and Germany itself. This reduced the supply of weapons to the fronts.

By 1944, 20% of German ammunition production and 30% of manufactured direct-fire weapons were destined for the anti-aircraft defense. Early 1944 the American P-51 Mustang became available, a long-range fighter that could escort bombers into Germany. In mid-1944 the Allies conquered France, which punched a hole in the German air defences and enabled them to use bases close to Germany.

The effectiveness of the carpet bombing was limited. They did not break the morale of the civilian population and the production of the German war industry continued to increase every year. It was not until the second half of 1944 that German industrial production fell sharply.

The air war required both sides to deploy large numbers of men and equipment. The Allies used Britain in 1944/1945 as an attack base for an air fleet of thirty thousand bombers and fighters, fifteen times the number available to the *Luftwaffe in* the West at the time. Allied losses were high at forty thousand planes, but their large production capacity compensated. The Germans lost a total of fifty thousand aircraft in this battle. The Allies dropped one and a half million tons of bombs on Germany, killing half a million German civilians.

Africa and the Mediterranean

Italy, with a weak army and limited industrial capacity, embarked on a series of military adventures in which only German help prevented rapid defeat. August 1940 it occupied British Somaliland. A British counter-offensive until November 1941 caused the loss of Italian Somaliland, Eritrea, and Abyssynia.

Two hundred thousand men invaded the British-controlled Kingdom of Egypt from Libya on 13 September 1940, threatening the Suez Canal and the oil fields of Iraq and Persia. The British conquered the east of Libya. The Italian fleet was largely eliminated. The German Afrika Korps under Erwin Rommel recaptured the Cyrenaica in early 1941.

After the area was lost to him again in late 1941, Rommel advanced first to Gazala in 1942 and then to El Alamein, only 106 kilometers west of Alexandria. He was unable to break through the British position there.

The Balkans

Albania had already been occupied by the Italians in April 1939. Mussolini, jealous of the German successes, started the Greco-Italian War on 28 October 1940.

The Italian offensive stalled and a Greek counter-offensive after 14 November 1940 threw the Italians well over the Albanian border. At first the Greeks refused British support, so as not to provoke Hitler. Only a small base was allowed on Crete.

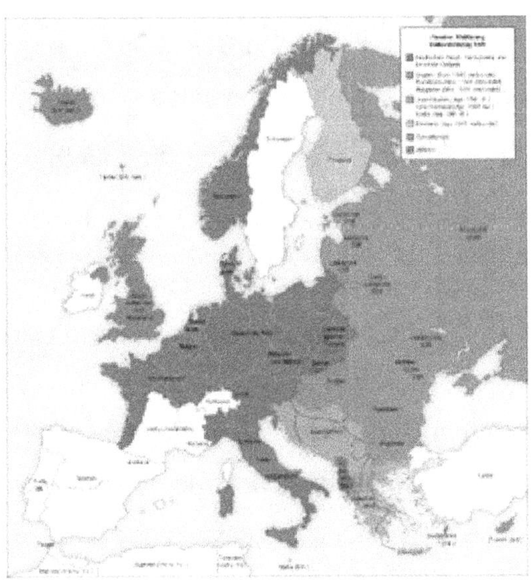

Germany began to make territorial changes in the Balkans.

The main victims were Romania, which had to cede Zevenburgen to Hungary, Bessarabia to the Soviet Union and the southern Dobroedzja to Bulgaria. Hungary, Romania, and Bulgaria were forced to join the Axis.After German troops entered Bulgaria, the Greeks allowed British troops to land on their mainland.

Yugoslavia also joined the Axis but on 27 March 1941 a coup occurred in response. In the Invasion of Yugoslavia, German, Italian, Hungarian and Bulgarian forces therefore overwhelmed the fragmented defenses of the Yugoslavs from 6 April 1941. At the same time, German forces invaded Greece from Bulgaria.

The Greeks failed to sufficiently reinforce the Metaxas Line and connect it to the Albanian front so that the Greek-British forces succumbed to German superiority. On 27 April 1941, Athens fell. On 20 May, German paratroopers landed on Crete, which they captured from the British after ten days of heavy fighting. Yugoslavia and Greece were divided. The campaign led to a delay in German preparations for the invasion of the Soviet Union.

The Axis Powers apparently controlled the Balkans, but would face fierce partisan fighting in Yugoslavia, Albania and Greece, which the Western Allies supported with arms supplies and bound many divisions. The nationalist and communist resistance movements also fought among themselves leading to the Greek Civil War which would last until 1949.

In Yugoslavia and Albania, the Communists were strong enough to drive the Germans out of large areas more or less on their own, allowing them to remain mavericks in the postwar Communist bloc. From Greece the Germans withdrew of their own accord in late 1944, when the advancing Red Army threatened to cut them off.

The Eastern Front

Between 1941 and 1945, the battle on the Eastern Front was the core conflict in Europe, in which the two largest European powers largely determined the outcome of the war. National Socialism wanted to gain *Lebensraum* by exterminating the Jews in the East, destroying communism and, according to the *Generalplan Ost*, permanently subjugating a depleted Slavic population to an upper layer of Germanic colonizers. More than an imperialist pursuit of territory or raw materials, it was an existential struggle to the death for both states.

The eastern front suffered most casualties, among civilians and soldiers. Of the 3 251 868 killed and missing in action in the German field army until 30 November 1944, after which there are no more exact data, 2 416 784 fell on the Eastern Front. This reflects the relative deployment of men, supplies and materiel.

On the eastern front Germany was defeated. Because the turnover on other fronts was much less and air force, anti-aircraft and naval forces took a third of the available soldiers, there was at any given moment only a minority of the total German strength in the east. Although the manpower of the Wehrmacht rose to almost ten million in 1943, the strength on the Eastern Front fell below three million, partly because most did everything they could to be deployed elsewhere. The Red Army recorded the deaths of 6 329 000 soldiers.

Operation Barbarossa

On 22 June 1941, the German army was at the height of its power as a mass of 153 divisions were at full strength and fully supplied and ready for the invasion of the Soviet Union.

More than three million German soldiers, equipped with 3580 tanks, 7184 guns and 2740 aircraft began Operation Barbarossa, supported by the Romanian and Finnish armies. The much larger Red Army of nearly six million soldiers, 25 700 tanks and 18 700 aircraft was the inferior in experience, competence, training, battle ability and logistical support. In the first phase, the Soviets made the mistake of trying to imitate German modern movement warfare instead of digging in or positioning themselves in depth. As a result, their border armies and mechanized corps were surrounded and destroyed within five weeks.

By the end of July, Germany seemed to have won the war against the Soviet Union - and with it the entire Second World War. Arms orders for the army were firmly reduced.

The German Army Group North now had to advance to Leningrad, Army Group South had to reach the oil fields in the Caucasus and Army Group Center had to conquer Moscow. Before October, the area west of the Volga had to be occupied before the autumn mud made the unpaved roads impassable. Significant resistance was no longer expected.

67

In fact, large Soviet armies were again formed on the line Luga - Smolensk - Kiev. They had seriously underestimated the mobilization capacity of the Red Army: it would call up almost thirty million reservists and recruits until the end of the war.

The setback led to a crisis in German command. The realization began to dawn that the battle would last not a few months but many years while the country was not prepared for a protracted war. The German army used the month of August to resupply and establish a new strategy.

Here a second threatening development occurred for the Germans: Hitler, though a total amateur, began to interfere increasingly with operational command. He ordered Army Group Central to turn south to join Army Group South in destroying the Soviet army near Kiev. When the troops were back in position, the offensive against Moscow got bogged down in mud in October. They did reach the Leningrad - Moscow - Rostov line during the early frosts, but then the poorly supplied troops were hit by the Russian cold, with no winter equipment. The Soviet Union's first real counter-offensive in December and January 1942 threw Army Group Middle back nearly two hundred kilometers.

On December 11, Hitler declared war on the United States of America. Within four months Germany had gone from a seemingly won position to a geostrategic disaster.

Stalingrad

The German army on the Eastern Front was permanently weakened in the winter of 1941/1942. German arms production increased only gradually and the tank strength would never again reach three thousand. The much larger Soviet arms industry, however, had been evacuated from Leningrad and Kharkov to the Urals and would produce twenty thousand tanks in 1942, of the superior types T-34 and KV-1. The new Soviet armies were mainly posted in front of Moscow. This left the southern sector worse occupied. Hitler ordered to break through this with about fifty divisions that were still on strength. In this way he hoped to conquer the oil fields in the Caucasus and gain both fuel and time to build up the German war industry. The German armoured units reached the Don in the summer of 1942 and then turned south for a distant march towards Baku, which would never be reached. They could no longer fulfil their role as an armoured reserve while the long flanks of their advance could only be covered by the deployment of inferior Italian, Hungarian and Romanian armies.

The situation became even riskier when Hitler ordered the capture of Stalingrad on the Volga, an important centre for the arms industry. The Sixth Army under Friedrich Paulus, in a pointless struggle for prestige, became embroiled in bloody urban combat. A pincer movement, cutting across flanking Romanian armies, surrounded a quarter of a million Sixth Army men in Operation Uranus in November 1942. An attempt at disengagement by armoured troops hastily recalled from the Caucasus failed and on 2 February 1943 the remnants capitulated. Never before had an entire German army been lost. Subsequent Soviet offensives also destroyed the Hungarian and Italian troops after which almost the entire area above the Caucasus had to be evacuated by the Germans and armoured forces advanced hundreds of kilometres to the west.

The loss of prestige for Germany was great. Joseph Goebbels proclaimed "total war", i.e. with even heavier burdens on the German population. The battle showed that the Red Army gradually acquired the operational capability to defeat the better trained German units with a numerical superiority of lower quality troops.

El Alamein, *Torch* and Italy

At the same time as the Battle of Stalingrad, Bernard Montgomery, significantly reinforced with American equipment, inflicted a devastating defeat on Rommel in the Second Battle of El Alamein in November 1942. That same month, British and American forces landed in Algeria and Morocco in Operation Torch. Rommel advanced west into Tunisia but the Axis forces were destroyed there in May 1943, driving them out of Africa entirely.

The Allies landed on Sicily on 10 July 1943, which led to the fall and arrest of Benito Mussolini on 25 July, after which the government of Pietro Badoglio secretly negotiated peace. On 3 September 1943 the Strait of Messina was crossed. Italy signed an armistice on 8 September and sided with the Allies on 13 October. The Germans had been occupying Italy according to *Fall Achse* since early August and encountered little Italian resistance. Some seven hundred thousand Italian prisoners of war were taken as slaves. German armoured units that resisted Operation Avalanche, the landing at Salerno, on 9 September, withdrew and, with reinforcements, formed a strong main front south of Rome. Attempts to break through at the Battle of Monte Cassino failed. However, the Germans felt compelled to evacuate Sardinia and Corsica in 1943. In January 1944 the Allies tried to attack the line in the back via the Landing at Anzio but it remained an isolated bridgehead. Only in May 1944 the line was broken and on 4 June 1944 Rome was liberated. After that the Germans blocked an advance northwards in the *Gotenstellung* which only fell in April 1945 after which the Germans capitulated in Italy on 30 April.

The Italian front seized some thirty German divisions, causing a serious weakening of the eastern front. On 12 September 1943 Mussolini was liberated by a German commando action and then led the Italian Social Republic, a rump state without the south and South Tyrol annexed to Germany. The ISR made only a minor war effort. On April 28, 1945, Mussolini was executed by partisans.

The Casablanca and Tehran Conferences

The great coalition that had formed in 1941 between the United Kingdom, the USSR and the United States had difficulty in arriving at a common strategy. There was always the threat that the Western Allies or the Soviet Union would make a separate peace with Germany.

A peace in the West would end the major Allied arms deliveries to the Red Army, provide Hitler with access to oil and resources, and free up millions of soldiers for a perhaps successful battle on the Eastern Front. Conversely, without such an Eastern Front, successful landings in Europe would become extremely problematic and the liberation of Western Europe doubtful.

Between the UK and the US there were also differences of opinion. They had already agreed on March 27, 1941 to give priority to the fight in Europe over the fight against Japan.

In 1942, however, Japan scored major victories, and Roosevelt desired a greater British contribution to the war in Asia and hoped to complete the final victory against Hitler as quickly as possible so that American forces would be freed up for fighting in the Pacific.

He planned to open a Second Front in 1943, something which Stalin also insisted on. The British, however, did not think this was realistic. Churchill wanted the "soft underbelly" of Europe to be attacked, first by a landing in Italy and then by a landing in the Balkans. He had always been a staunch anti-communist and hoped to prevent Soviet domination of Eastern Europe. Churchill was not averse to a separate peace with Germany, provided Hitler was overthrown.

In January 1943, at the Casablanca Conference, the differences between the Western Allies were partially resolved. First they would conquer Tunisia and land in Italy but then in France and not in the Balkans.

Efforts were made to reconcile de Gaulle's Free French and the French authorities in North Africa so that very gradually France would regain the role of full partner in the war, something facilitated by the fact that Germany had occupied France after *Torch* Vichy. Roosevelt included in the Declaration of Casablanca the demand for an "unconditional surrender" of the Axis powers, which virtually ruled out a separate peace.

Stalin had not been present in Casablanca. In November 1943, he met Churchill and Roosevelt at the Tehran Conference. Churchill agreed to a landing in France in May 1944, the end for his plans in the Balkans. Stalin promised a major summer offensive for that year. Churchill and Stalin reached an agreement about the new borders of Poland. They also agreed to divide Germany. Roosevelt suggested the formation of a United Nations. This way, he made Stalin enthusiastic for the idea to divide the world after the war in two power blocks, which could exist peacefully next to each other.

Kursk and the Ukraine

The collapse of the German front in the Ukraine made Hitler realise that he had to place operational command on the Eastern Front in the hands of a professional. In a brilliant campaign, Von Manstein destroyed the Red Army's armoured spearheads throughout February and March 1943 and stabilised the situation, recapturing Kharkov. It would remain the last major German victory of the war. During 1943 German tank production increased.

Guderian urged Hitler to form a large armored reserve in the east of about two thousand tanks. If an equal number could be gathered in the west, there was good hope to repel any Allied attack. This was linked to the creation of balanced armoured grenadier divisions, in which infantry, equipped with half-tracks, worked closely together with tanks and dive-bombers.

Hitler, however, gave priority to his political objectives. Afraid of a coup by the generals, he allowed the Waffen-SS to develop into a parallel army. This manpower could have been used much more efficiently by bringing the structurally understaffed regular divisions up to strength.

The SS stressed the supposed value of a fanatical National Socialist "will to conquer" over professionalism. This will had to justify Hitler's order to hold out even when retreat was the only sensible option.

After Stalingrad, Hitler wanted to remove the impression that Germany had already lost the war. For this purpose it was necessary to carry out a large summer offensive, just as in 1941 and 1942. The front arc near Kursk was chosen as the start of that operation. Germany had developed a new generation of tanks in response to the T-34: the Tiger I and Panther. These types were expensive to produce and Hitler postponed the attack until more of them became available. This enabled the Red Army to build wide defensive belts of anti-tank artillery near Kursk.

In the Battle of Kursk in July 1943, this last major attack by the Germans ran aground. They lost the strategic initiative and the chance to defend themselves effectively forever. Their number of operational tanks dropped to a thousand, insufficient to close their weak lines, occupied by undermanned infantry divisions still dependent on horse transport, after a breakthrough by enemy tank armies.

In September the German army fled to the Dnieper. It hoped to build an *Ostwall* at the wide stream behind which they could recover. The Soviet command realised that this had to be prevented at all costs. The Red Army crossed the river and until April 1944 carried out a series of offensives in which a massive deployment of men and tanks drove the Germans out of the western Ukraine. Hitler forbade bringing armoured divisions from France for fear this was part of a plan to overthrow him. His only hope was to make the "invasion" fail. His ban on retreating led to unnecessarily heavy German losses.

Landing in Normandy

Until the summer of 1944, the large armies and material reserves the Western Allies had built up had hardly been deployed. They could only become a decisive factor after an invasion of Western Europe.

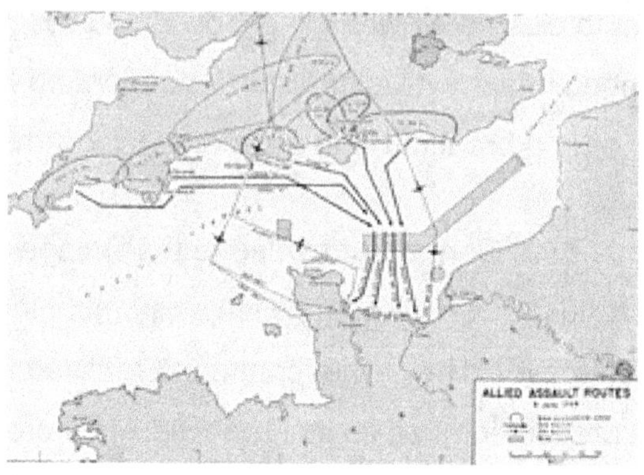

For a successful defense of Germany it was essential that such a landing would fail. However, because of the losses on the Eastern Front, Hitler had accumulated in France only half of the armor reserves needed, despite increased tank production. Allied air superiority would make it difficult to move those reserves. Rommel hoped to drive the landing forces into the sea in the first 24 hours because the defensive line on the west coast, the *Atlantic Wall*, had
81

little depth. However, one did not dare to guess where exactly the landings would take place and the reserves were scattered.

On 6 June 1944, *D-Day*, Operation Overlord began, the largest combined amphibious and airborne operation in history with more than six thousand vessels, supported by twelve thousand aircraft, landing in five bridgeheads on the coast of Normandy. The Allies won the battle of attrition with the slowly arriving German reserves because of their material reserves. In late July 1944 the Americans broke out into Operation Cobra, covering the German main front from the west. Hitler forbade a retreat and the German

82

forces in Normandy were largely destroyed. On 15 August the Allies landed in southern France, in Operation Dragoon, and advanced rapidly northwards. Paris was liberated by the Free French on 25 August 1944. The German army fled to the north-east. By early September, France and Belgium were largely liberated.

Operation Bagration

After D-Day a major part of the German armoured divisions from the east was moved to France. The German eastern front was now very vulnerable. The loss of the western Ukraine had stretched the front line to about four thousand kilometers. What armoured reserves remained had to be placed in southern Poland to prevent the Red Army from advancing to the Baltic Sea in one go. Army Group Central, which had seventy tanks left, was attacked on 22 June 1944 in Operation Bagration and practically destroyed within a month. Belarus was liberated and the advance finally isolated Army Group North in Courland.

Finland ended all acts of war against the Soviet Union on 5 September. On 20 August, the Red Army opened a major offensive against Romania. Two German armies were surrounded and destroyed, after which the country chose the Allied side. This deprived Germany of the only major source of oil. On 5 September, the Soviet Union declared war on Bulgaria, which immediately ceased all resistance. The Red Army crossed the Carpathians and advanced on Budapest.

Delay in the Allied advance

The catastrophes of the summer of 1944 had caused irreparable damage to the Wehrmacht. In Normandy and on the eastern front 130 divisions had been destroyed or isolated. The fronts could only be closed by deploying barely trained recruits, which seriously reduced the quality of the fighting units.

This was all the worse because the armies of the Western Allies consisted of elite divisions: fully motorized and amply armored. Yet this did not lead to the instant collapse of Nazi Germany. The Allied advance stalled and only resumed in early 1945.

This was partly due to desperate emergency measures taken by the regime. After the assassination of Hitler there was a paranoid atmosphere of terror and any alleged sign of resistance or unwillingness could be punished with death.

Women were required to work more and every man or boy who could carry a weapon was drafted into the *Volkssturm*. However, the main reason for the delay lay in major logistical problems: after the intense fighting, the Allied troops had to be resupplied and, because of the large amount of ground gained over longer supply lines, in the west all the way from Normandy.

On 17 September, the British and Americans in Operation Market Garden attempted to quickly exploit German weakness. Airborne landings had to take the bridges over the major Dutch rivers to the Rhine bridge at Arnhem to circumvent the Westwall and push through to the Ruhr area. This failed and only through the bloody Battle of the Scheldt in the autumn could the Allies clear the sea route to the vital port of Antwerp. In December 1944 Hitler gambled away his last armoured reserve to the Ardennes Offensive to retake Antwerp; this delayed the renewed

Allied attack by only six weeks. German propaganda about *Wunderwaffen* suggested that a last-ditch effort could buy time for the deployment of atomic weapons, but in fact the V1, a "flying bomb," and the ballistic missile V2 could only be equipped with conventional warheads that inflicted several thousand civilian casualties mainly in London and Antwerp.

1945

January 1945, the Red Army opened the Wisła-Oder Offensive with the largest concentration of men and materiel of the war. Because Hitler had squandered his armour reserve on the Ardennes Offensive, the attack could not be absorbed and the German army in Poland was crushed, with the Soviets advancing as far as Berlin.

The battle was prolonged because, fearing flank attacks, they first purged Silesia, East Prussia and Pomerania in March. Meanwhile, Hitler launched some fruitless attacks in Hungary. These only led to the exhaustion of his troops. Vienna was quickly taken and politicians there proclaimed another independent Austria. In April 1945, a pincer movement surrounded the German capital in the Battle of Berlin.

In February 1945, the British and Americans conquered the Rhineland. The Rhine did not prove to be an insurmountable obstacle.

On 7 March 1945 the Americans captured the Ludendorff Bridge at Remagen and on 24 March Allied troops crossed the Rhine at Wesel in Operation Plunder, the last major airborne landing of the war. The German defences in the west collapsed as a result. The Wehrmacht announced that in this way they wanted to spare as many civilians as possible from the revenge of the Red Army.

In the Netherlands, however, Dutch SS officers continued to defend Holland and Utrecht, exacerbating the winter of starvation. Hitler issued the "Nero decrees" to destroy the country in order to deny the inferior German people any possibility of survival after the war, but they could not be implemented on a large scale. Americans and Russians shook hands in Torgau on the Elbe on 25 April 1945. Hitler, realizing that all was lost, committed suicide in his

89

surrounded Berlin bunker on April 30, 1945. On May 1, 1945, German radio announced that the Führer had died at the head of his troops defending Berlin. With this last lie, Nazi Germany went down. The troops in the Netherlands surrendered on 5 May. The general surrender was signed by representatives of Karl Dönitz's government on 7/9 May 1945.

After the countries of Central America and Brazil had preceded them, most South American countries declared war on Germany in early 1945, as did Turkey. Participation in the war was initially a condition for becoming a member of the United Nations, which was founded in April. At the Yalta Conference from February 7 to 11, 1945, during which Roosevelt, Churchill and Stalin made many formal and informal arrangements about the postwar situation, the Soviet Union had agreed to participate in the UN, with separate seats for Belarus and Ukraine.

Economic comparison

The course of the war was complexly linked to the relative production of weapons. At the beginning of the war Germany was already behind the Allies in this respect. It was only successful because of its tactical superiority.

The imbalance was at its worst in 1942. In a short time, a military-industrial complex had been created in the US that produced twice as much as the Axis powers put together. Large industrial companies were given the freedom to regulate the economy. Total industrial production rose by a quarter a year, to more than double by the end of the war.

The Soviet planned economy allowed for similar growth in the arms industry in 1942, albeit at the expense of the rest of consumption. Due to the strategic situation, however, Germany managed to hold its own in 1942 and 1943. By 1944, Germany had largely caught up. However, it was unable to build up reserves due to strategic mistakes, while German forces were handicapped by fuel shortages. D-Day brought the US armies onto the battlefield and Germany's tactical advantage fell away, sealing its defeat.

Hitler and his allies in Europe controlled in 1942 an area, the *Großraum*, with more inhabitants than the Soviet Union and the US together and with an economic production equal to that of the Americans. That potential, however, was poorly exploited and as a whole hardly grew.

Because of the earlier neglect of the railways, the Germans were forced to steal locomotives from other countries, which seriously reduced the transport capacity of the occupied territories. The stagnating production of coal, by far the most important source of energy, could thus no longer be efficiently distributed. Most of the allies were technically and socially underdeveloped and their populations could not easily be used for the German war effort.

The Low Countries and France made a substantial contribution in 1941, but much of their manpower was then forced to do forced labour in Germany so that more Germans could enlist, an inefficient system. The mass extermination of prisoners of war, forced labourers and Jews destroyed even more manpower. Germany had no real planned economy.

As the NSDAP increasingly took over society, ministries lost their de facto power and the civil service became ineffective. The party itself fell apart into warring factions that all competed for Hitler's favour. Industrialists joined in and tried to obtain money and resources with spectacular but impractical designs.

Agricultural production faltered and the whole continent was on the brink of famine if there were crop failures. Even before the invasion of the Soviet Union, Herbert Backe had calculated that only the starvation of the urban population could provide a food surplus for Germany.

However, this *Hunger Plan* could not be implemented systematically and the area could not even feed the German occupation forces. In general, the occupied territories cost Germany more than they yielded.

The relative tank production of Germany and the Soviet Union can serve as an example of developments.

Germany produced many aircraft but the production of the Axis powers was far behind the total aircraft production of the Allies.

The war in Asia

Japan in the first half of the 20th century

Japan modernised radically during the Meiji period in the second half of the 19th century. However, the new industrial power lacked natural resources. Between 1859 and 1942, Japan pursued an imperialist policy of securing supplies of raw materials and food by conquering and controlling neighbouring countries. To this end, a strong army and one of the largest navies in the world were created.

Victories in the First Sino-Japanese War (1894-1895) and Russo-Japanese War (1904-1905) resulted in Japanese control of Taiwan to the south, Korea and Manchuria to the west, and South Sakhalin to the north. In 1919 Japan gained control of the vast South Pacific Mandate area. The introduction of universal suffrage in 1925 provoked a conservative reaction that increasingly undermined parliamentary democracy.

The Japanese imperialist drive was revived by the Great Depression after 1929. The military began to increasingly determine foreign policy. Between 1932 and 1936 the country was ruled by admirals. After the failed coup in Japan on February 26, 1936, the army enforced that the minister of war would always be a serving general. After that, the country was effectively a military dictatorship.

The Second Sino-Japanese War

With the National Protection War of 1915, central authority in China lost power to regional warlords. Japan gained more influence as a result and forced the weak Chinese government into "unequal treaties". The treaties were poorly enforced: a weak government could not enforce them and a strong one had no interest in doing so.

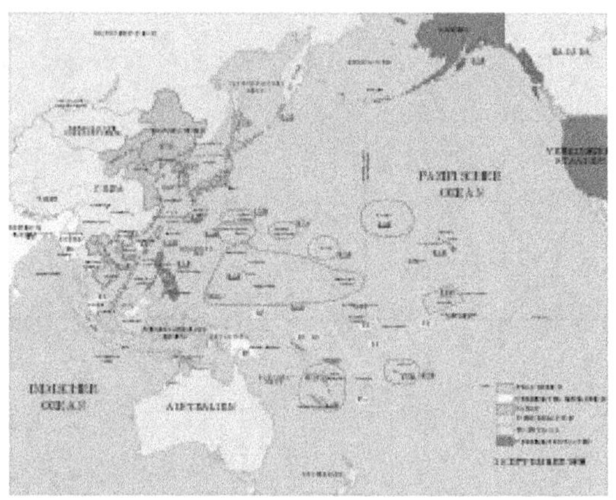

After bringing the warlords in southern and central China under his control, Chiang Kai-shek, the leader of the Kwomintang, led the Northern Expedition in 1927 and 1928 against the bosses of the northern warlords in

Beijing. When Zhang Xueliang, the warlord who controlled Manchuria, declared his allegiance to Chiang, the Japanese intervened. They created a satellite state of Manchukwo in 1931 under the last Chinese emperor Pu Yi. Japan withdrew from the League of Nations which condemned this action. Chiang attacked until 1936, with German help, mainly the Communists whom he expelled from southern China. Japan began to control the warlords in the north.

In late 1936, Chiang was kidnapped by Zhang Xueliang, the Xi'an Incident, and forced to ally with the Communists against the Japanese. Officers of the Kwantung Army therefore provoked, without the knowledge of the Japanese Supreme Command, the Marco Polo Bridge Incident on July 7, 1937, as a pretext to occupy northeastern China.

This Second Sino-Japanese War is considered in Asian perspective as the beginning of the Second World War. Chiang remained fiercely opposed to the invasion. Japan attacked its capital in late 1937, resulting in the Nanking Massacre with three hundred thousand civilian casualties. Millions of peasants were killed by terror, floods and famine. Japan was unable to defeat China or to profitably exploit the occupied territories.

The road to Pearl Harbor

In 1938 a border war ensued between Japan and the Soviet Union which occupied Xinjiang and supported its communist satellite state of Mongolia. In August 1939, General Zhukov won a decisive victory over the Japanese in the Battle of Halhin Gol, after which Japan abandoned its pursuit of northern territorial expansion. The political influence of the Northern Assault Group, the exponent of the Japanese Army, diminished in favor of the Southern Assault Group, the favorite of the Japanese Navy. When Germany invaded the Soviet Union, Japan remained neutral, considering a good relationship with Stalin as backing for a southern attack.

In 1940 Japan signed with Germany and Italy the Three-Power Pact, a treaty of assistance. After the German conquest of the Netherlands and France, the United States feared that Japan would exploit this by taking over the western colonies in South-East Asia. September 1940 Vichy-France was indeed forced to bring the north of Indochina under Japanese control. As punishment, the US, UK and the Dutch government in exile, which still controlled the oil wells in the Dutch East Indies, instituted an oil and steel boycott against Japan. The Japanese military under Admiral Isoroku Yamamoto started to prepare a campaign to drive the United States out of the Pacific Ocean. July 1941 also occupied the south of Indo-China.

Unlike the Germans, the Japanese military leadership, government and emperor were well aware that such a struggle would ultimately be futile. Despite a strong industrial base, a war of attrition against the world's largest economy was bound to be lost.

101

Doing nothing was not an option because the country would have collapsed economically and militarily because of the boycott, due to a lack of raw materials and oil, 90% of which was imported. Complying with US demands would undoubtedly lead to further diplomatic pressure to withdraw from China.

Such a loss of face would not be compatible with the army's honour. Rather, they accepted the great risk of a heroic military defeat, comforting themselves with the small chance of gaining an economic base through the conquest of oil fields in Southeast Asia, including the Dutch East Indies, that would force the U.S. into a settlement after a devastating attack on Pearl Harbor.

The Japanese offensive

In 1941, Japan had the largest fleet of flying camp ships in
the world. They carried out a surprise attack on Pearl
Harbour in the Hawaiian archipelago on 7 December 1941.
The American battle fleet was largely knocked out, but the
three flying camp ships survived because they happened
to be on exercise.

At the same time attacks started against British Malacca
and the American colony the Philippines. On December
11, Hitler declared war on the United States, hoping they
would be kept busy by the Japanese for the time being.

103

After a brief invasion Thailand abandoned all resistance and sided with the Japanese in January 1942. The British battleship *Prince of Wales* and the battle cruiser *Repulse* were sunk by bombers off the coast of Malacca on 10 December. The Allies now had no battleships left on this battlefield.

The relatively small Allied colonial garrisons conducted a passive defence and were rolled up piece by piece. Hong Kong fell on December 25, 1941. The Japanese landed on the east coast of Malacca and attacked the large British naval base from the landward side in the Battle of Singapore.

On 15 February 1942 the 130 000 British, Indian and Australian troops surrendered. The American bases on Guam and Wake were lost. Japanese invasions of Burma, the Solomon Islands, the Dutch East Indies and New Guinea followed in January. Manila, Kuala Lumpur and Rabaul were captured by Japan. The American garrison in the Philippines withdrew to the Bataan peninsula but was forced to surrender in April. Bali and Timor fell in February 1942; Rangoon and Java in March. An attempt by Allied light cruisers to stop the Japanese landing fleet failed in the Battle of the Java Sea.

Mandalay followed in early May. The Japanese air force eventually controlled the airspace completely and carried out bombing raids on northern Australia. The Doolittle Raid of April 1942 in which the Americans bombed Tokyo was only a symbolic act.

The tide is turning

After their first war aims had been achieved, the Japanese were in doubt about further strategy. Air station ships had become the decisive factor in naval warfare. Before their construction program would give the Americans an advantage, the Japanese wanted to conquer as much territory as possible. First they attacked to the west. On 5 April 1942, five air camp ships attacked Colombo.

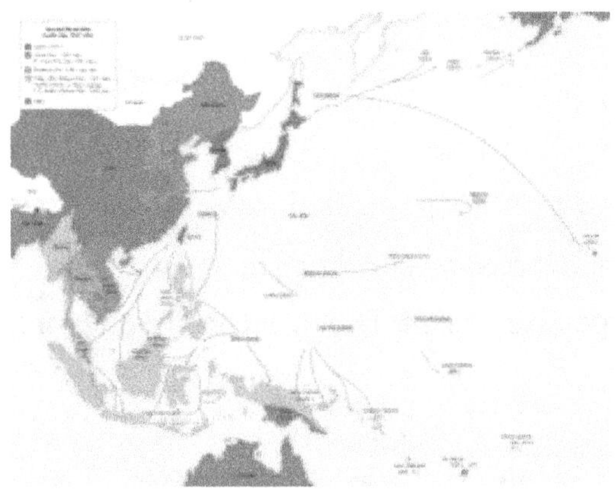

The British fleet withdrew from Ceylon but on 9 April the airship *HMS Hermes* was sunk. Japan, however, refrained from attempting contact with the Axis powers in the Middle East. Attention was shifted to the south. The conquest of

Australia and New Zealand would weaken the British empire, deprive the Allies of a base for counterattack and sever their east-west connections.

However, the Japanese navy did not realize that the Americans had broken its codes. While supporting a preliminary amphibious assault on Port Moresby, in eastern New Guinea, in May 1942 during the Battle of the Coral Sea, they were ambushed by two American carrier ships, the first time in history that *carrier fleets* fought a battle.

Although the *USS Lexington (CV-2)* sank, the Japanese lost the *Shoho*. Worse was that almost all the pilots of the *Zuikaku* and the *Shokaku*, their two most modern flying camp ships, were killed. The invasion of Port Moresby was called off.

In early June, the four remaining large flying camp ships attacked Midway as a prelude to a conquest of the entire Hawaiian archipelago, followed by a destruction of the California wharves and the locks of the Panama Canal to impede an American fleet buildup in the Pacific.

107

Once again they were ambushed. Dive bombers from three American flying camp ships, the USS *Yorktown*, the USS *Enterprise*, and the USS *Hornet*, plunged the *Kaga*, the *Akagi*, the *Soryu*, and the *Hiryu* on June 4 and 5.

This Battle of Midway, despite the loss of the *Yorktown*, was the turning point in the war in Asia. It would take Japan nearly three years to replace the four sunken ships.

During the same period the American shipyards launched sixteen large flying camp ships, in addition to nine light flying camp ships and, for their own navy, fifty-four *escort carriers*.

Guadalcanal and *Island Hopping*

Neither Japan nor the US were capable of major offensives in mid-1942. The Imperial Navy continued to attempt to advance towards Australia. A land attack from the north towards Port Moresby was blocked by the Australians along the *Kokoda Track*. In August 1942 the first Japanese landing failed, in the Battle of Milne Bay.

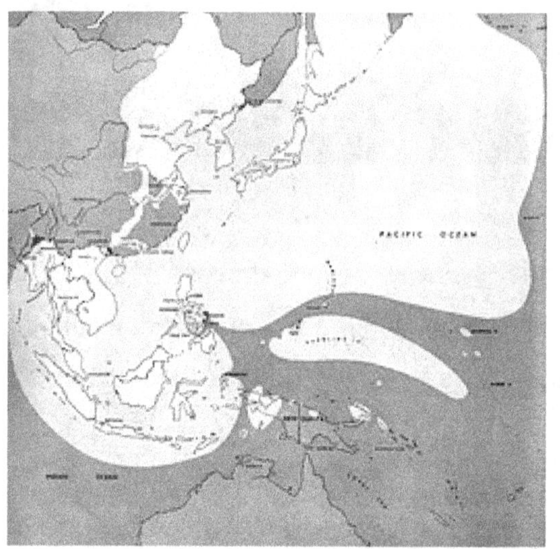

That same month, both the Americans and Japanese landed on Guadalcanal, one of the Solomon Islands. This began the six-month Battle of Guadalcanal, part of the

Battle of the Solomon Islands. In numerous fleet actions, the Japanese gradually lost ground, despite sacrificing many ships and men. In 1943 the Americans and Australians established the bridgeheads Buna and Gona on the northeast coast of New Guinea.

The Americans were able to set an aggressive strategy in 1943 after rapidly converting cruisers to light flying camp ships. To defeat Japan, it was not necessary to recapture all of Southeast Asia. It would suffice to take the north of the Philippines to break the supply line to oil from Sumatra.

This attack from the east was to take place over two axes. Douglas MacArthur was to advance west across the New Guinea zone with a southern axis.

As the northern axis, Admiral Chester Nimitz wanted to quickly take strategic islands in an *island hopping* or *leapfrogging* campaign, passing powerful Japanese garrisons and isolating them, in order to gain control of the archipelagoes south of Japan.

The Japanese brought in additional troops to cordon off these offensives in a "blockade strategy," hoping to gain at least six months to strengthen their fleet, air force, and garrisons.

The southern assault began in June 1943 with a bloody capture of New Georgia. In August followed a landing on Bougainville, which would not be taken until 1945. Given the tough Japanese resistance McArthur decided to play leapfrog and passed the Japanese main force at Rabaul on New Britain. By the spring of 1944 he had extended his control over the entire northern coast of New Guinea, taking positions up to three thousand kilometers west of Guadalcanal.

November 1943 the northern attack started with landings in the Gilberts Islands. After heavy fighting Tarawa was

111

taken. In the winter of 1944 they penetrated the Marshall Islands, quickly capturing Majuro, Kwajalein and Eniwetok.

Reconquest of the Philippines

In the late spring of 1944 both sides prepared for the *Kantai Kessen*, the "decisive naval battle". The two years of preparation time had been poorly used by the Japanese. There had been no industrial capacity to produce a new generation of tanks so that Japanese armored vehicles now lagged far behind the American in armor and firepower. The handful of new flying camp ships were dwarfed by the American *Big Blue Fleet*. They had failed to fully train enough Navy pilots because the first batch had been sent to the garrison at Rabaul. American submarines sunk so many merchant ships that the supply of raw materials and oil was seriously reduced. Therefore from April 1944 Operation Ichi-Go was carried out, the biggest offensive of the Japanese army during the war, across South China to establish a land connection with Indo-China. In the spring a serious attempt was made to invade India from Burma, in Operation U-Go. This was repulsed and the British, Indians and Chinese would gradually reconquer Burma during 1944 and 1945.

June 1944 the American Fifth Fleet attacked the Mariana Islands with seven large flying camp ships. On 15 June they landed on Saipan. The Imperial Navy was now steaming eastward with five large carrier battleships, on 19 and 20 June entering the Battle of the Philippine Sea, the largest naval battle ever fought between *carrier fleets*. It turned out to be a bitter disappointment. Not a single American carrier ship was hit. Over four hundred of the Japanese naval pilots were shot down. American submarines sank the air camp ships *Shokaku* and *Taiho*. The defeat was hidden from the public and never again would Japanese *carriers* engage in regular battle with the Americans. Between 21 July and 10 August Guam was recaptured in the Mariana Islands. On 24 November 1944, long-range B-29 Superfortress bombers began bombing Japan from Saipan, reinforced in late February 1945 by two airfields on Guam.

The Americans first considered to conquer Formosa, but only a quick end of the war in Europe would free the necessary forces. Therefore on 17 October 1944 the recapture of the Philippines was started by landings near and on Leyte. The Japanese navy now drew its last trump card: the battle fleet that was to defeat the Americans by ingenious strategy in the greatest naval battle in history, the Battle of the Gulf of Leyte. The last flying camp ships, without aircraft, lured the American Third Fleet to the north and a squadron of battleships lured the American Seventh Fleet to the south so that a middle squadron through the San Bernardino Strait could overrun the American landing fleet. This plan succeeded but after sinking an *escort carrier*, the central *task force withdrew* so the sacrifice of four air camp ships and three battleships had been in vain. On 9 January 1945 the Americans landed on Luzon which had been largely brought under control in the spring of 1945.

In November 1944, the Japanese began combining their numerous outdated aircraft and poorly trained pilots into the *Kamikaze*: suicide attacks by having the aircraft bore itself into an enemy ship with bomb and all. The 3912 suicide pilots sank 47 ships, including three *escort carriers*. Since nearly four hundred ships were also damaged, the phenomenon was seen as a serious problem. It reflected the habit of cornered Japanese infantry units not to surrender but to fight to the death in banzai attacks.

1945 in Asia

In the winter of 1945, the Allies severed virtually all maritime links between Japan and the South. Navy and industry suffered from an acute fuel shortage. Raw materials could only be obtained from Manchuria and guerrilla-ravaged China. Submarines broke up those routes as well.

More than a million tons of ships were sunk. Not only industrial production but also food production dropped to one third. To starve the population even more, after 27 March 1945 B-29s in Operation Starvation laid more than twelve thousand sea mines in Japanese coastal waters.

Bombing from the Marianas was intensified. The Japanese infrastructure was systematically destroyed. In the absence of good information about the industrial targets, there was a switch to terror bombing of Japanese cities; this left half a million dead and five million Japanese homeless. On 10 March 1945 the bombing of Tokyo took place, with at least 83 600 dead, and according to some estimates two hundred thousand, the heaviest in history.

In order to acquire bases closer to Japan for fighter planes to escort the bombers, the Landing on Iwo Jima was carried out, capturing the island between 19 February and 26 March, and the Battle of Okinawa between 1 April and 22 June, after a landing only slightly smaller than D-Day. The islands were doggedly defended, resulting in twenty thousand American deaths and over one hundred and thirty thousand Japanese, including on Okinawa many women who committed suicide for fear of rape.

On April 12, 1945, President Roosevelt died, with no weakening of the American war effort. By July 1945, the Japanese military strategic situation was hopeless. Allied flying camp ships eliminated nearly all remaining major Japanese warships in home waters between July 24 and

117

28 during massive attacks on the naval port of Kure.
Battleships like the USS *Missouri* and the *King George V*,
destroyed the coal and steel industry with impunity in July
and August with their accurate artillery, a sign to the
population that the situation was critical.

There were "doves" in the cabinet of the new Prime
Minister Admiral Kantarō Suzuki who hoped to negotiate a
surrender through the still neutral Soviet Union. The
"hawks," however, feared that such a move would lead to
demilitarization, punishment of war criminals, and the
abolition of the emperorship.

118

They thought they would gain a better bargaining position by repelling an expected landing on Kyushu with three thousand kamikaze pilots. On 26 July, the Allies repeated their demand for unconditional surrender in the Potsdam Declaration, without mentioning the Emperor. Since Okinawa, the Americans had feared that if they conquered Japan they would lose a million men. It came as a relief that the secret Manhattan Project successfully tested a first atomic bomb on July 16, 1945. President Harry S. Truman ordered the deployment of the new atomic weapon.

On August 6, 1945, the B-29 *Enola Gay dropped* a uranium bomb that destroyed Hiroshima, killing 79,000 people instantly. Still the Japanese cabinet made no decision to surrender, hoping that the Americans possessed only one such weapon. On August 9, a plutonium bomb destroyed Nagasaki, directly killing 39 000 people. Another 145 000 people succumbed to burns and radiation sickness after the two attacks.

The Soviet Union, under great American pressure, had agreed at the Yalta Conference to attack Japan no later than three months after the German surrender, on condition that it be allowed to conquer and annex South

119

Sakhalin and the Kurils. On August 9, 1945, "Operation August Storm" began, crushing the Japanese Kwantung army in Manchuria.

On 10 August Emperor Hirohito forced the Cabinet to send telegrams to the Allies that the Potsdam Declaration would be accepted provided his position remained unchanged. On August 11, the Allies circumvented this issue by stating that the Japanese people would be allowed to determine their own form of state. On August 15, 12:00, the emperor surrendered Japan in a radio address. This prevented the dropping of a third atomic bomb around August 19. On September 2, 1945 the capitulation was signed, on the battleship USS *Missouri*. Japan came under American occupation, led by MacArthur. President Truman declared a formal "cessation of hostilities" between the U.S. and Japan on December 31, 1946. On April 28, 1952, the San Francisco Peace Treaty was signed between Japan and most of the Allies. The exception was the Soviet Union because of a continuing dispute over the Kurils.

Casualties and warfare

The Second World War was characterized by the apparent impotence of the various pre-war peace and non-aggression treaties, as well as by an unprecedented mass and indiscriminate violence, with countless civilian victims. Previous wars had generally made a fundamental distinction between civilians and soldiers, with civilians being spared as much as possible or at least not being a primary target. This principle was widely abandoned during the Second World War; all parties now regarded each other's civilians as valid targets, arguing that civilians also contributed to the enemy's war effort. World War II is thus to this day the most telling example of total war. In addition, both Nazi Germany and the Soviet Union were totalitarian regimes, sustained by political repression and indoctrination. War between militaries was also distinctly harsh, especially on the Eastern Front. The internationally agreed rules of warfare (laid down in the Geneva Convention) were systematically and extensively violated, especially with regard to the treatment of prisoners of war.

Between 50 and 70 million people died during the Second World War. About two thirds of all victims were civilians, of whom it is estimated that more than 11 million belonged to minorities that were systematically persecuted and murdered. It was also the first - and so far the only - war in which nuclear weapons were used. At the end of the war, missile weapons and fighter jets were also used on a relatively small scale. During the war, all parties involved feared the use of chemical weapons, as had happened during the First World War. However, poison gas was only used on the periphery, namely by Italy in Abyssinia during the Second Italo-Ethiopian War and by Japan in China, where experiments with biological warfare also took place.

Persecution and destruction

An estimated 11 million people were systematically murdered, most of them in the concentration and extermination camps, which were run as a large-scale and efficient industry.

The unfortunates who were inferior and parasitic in the eyes of the Nazis had to be literally exterminated.

During the Holocaust, between five and six million Jews were murdered, as well as approximately five million gypsies, prisoners of war, slaves, disabled people, resistance fighters, Jehovah's witnesses, homosexuals, and dissidents. Various methods were used by the Germans to murder the *Untermenschen*, the gas chambers being the best known.

Civilian casualties and bombings

The warring parties deliberately bombed the civilian population. The Japanese carried out terror attacks on Shanghai, Wuhan, Nanking and Canton (Guangzhou), among others.

In Europe, the Germans bombarded Warsaw, Rotterdam, London and Coventry. The bombing was mainly used by the Allies as a means to bring the opponent to his knees.

The continuous bombing raid on Germany and Japan had two strategic goals: destruction of the war industry and damage to morale. However, the technique for aiming bombs was still so primitive that the war industry could only be damaged if huge areas were targeted, causing many civilian casualties.

Moreover, the Germans managed to place a significant part of the war industry in underground factories: until the very end of the war the Nazis were able to maintain an astonishing production capacity for war materiel. In Germany major cities like Hamburg, Cologne, Berlin and Dresden were heavily damaged, resulting in a total of 1.5 million dead and wounded.

In Japan, 67 cities with predominantly wooden houses were virtually wiped out by firebombs. This resulted in 500,000 deaths and 5 million homeless.

In the front zone of the Soviet Union, civilians had a very hard time. Nazi doctrine had little regard for the lives of the conquered Slavic people, who were considered a collection of Untermenschen; the government considered their survival secondary to achieving victory.

As a result, a total of about 11.9 million Soviet citizens died from war violence, terror, hunger, disease, and other hardships. But the Soviet Union did not spare its own citizens: anyone suspected of collaboration or insufficient support for the resistance was deported or executed.

French civilians also suffered great losses during the war. A total of 70,000 civilians died in France as a result of Allied actions, mostly bombings. A large part of them, 19,890 killed and a much larger number wounded, became casualties during the liberation of Normandy.

That number comes on top of the 15,000 French killed and 19,000 wounded during the bombing that served to prepare for Operation Overlord in the first five months of 1944. In total, more French civilians were killed by Allied action than British civilians were killed by German bombing.

Finally, in August 1945 nuclear weapons were used against the Japanese civilian population. There were approximately 250,000 direct victims.

Geopolitical implications

The world of 1939 had six major regional powers: the United States, emerging as a new superpower, the Communist Soviet Union, National Socialist Germany, Imperial Japan, and the colonial United Kingdom and France. This world was gone. The postwar period was characterized, until 1989 with the fall of the Berlin Wall, by the rivalry between two remaining superpowers: the United States and the Soviet Union.The mutual geopolitical rivalry between these two superpowers is known as the Cold War.

The rise of the two superpowers went hand in hand with the diminished power and position of the other three countries. Japan and Germany had lost the war, so their political and military global role was over for the time being.

In 1949 Germany was divided into a western and a smaller eastern part, which became part of NATO and the Warsaw Pact respectively. This would remain so until 1990. Japan remained undivided and was even allowed to keep its emperor, although he had to renounce his divine status. As

129

a protégé of the US, Japan could concentrate on economic reconstruction, which it did very successfully.

Apart from Hawaii, the United States had not experienced any war on its own soil and had suffered relatively light losses.

They supported the non-communist countries in Europe and Asia, both friendly countries and former enemies Germany and Japan, with tens of billions of dollars (Marshall Plan) and partly because of this, both the Japanese and the Western Europeans were able to work themselves out of the quagmire economically fast.

Things were different in the Soviet-dominated countries of Eastern Europe: instead of credit, they were given a Stalin-imposed communist economic model, which is why to this day Western Europeans are richer than Eastern Europeans.

The Second World War also set in motion a new wave of decolonisation. Although the British Empire was one of the winners, its decline as a great power soon began. The French and Dutch colonial empires also appeared to have had their day. The Japanese had stirred up nationalistic sentiments in the Far East to gain support in their struggle against the Western powers. This genie was out of the bottle and would not return.

Moreover, the British had exhausted most of their financial reserves to buy arms and supplies from the United States, which they had paid for with debt securities that would take them decades to repay. The colonial empires were crumbling rapidly, and after the Suez Crisis of 1956, France and the United Kingdom had to learn to live with medium power status.

Shortly after the war the state of Israel was founded in the British Mandate area of Palestine. This sowed the seeds for the Arab-Israeli conflict, as a result of which armed conflicts regularly flare up in this part of the Middle East to this day.

The horrors of the Second World War led to intensified international cooperation, particularly on the European continent. This led to the creation of the United Nations and, partly due to the Cold War, the European Union.

131

The success of the European Union, with its supranational

legislation, common currency and democratic values,

makes it difficult to imagine a European conflict today.